WORLD WAR I

FRANKLIN WATTS

New York   Chicago   London   Sydney
A First Book

FOR NICK

Photographs copyright ©: The Bettmann Archive, cover, 38 (top & bottom), 49, 51 (top); Culver Pictures, 2, 11, 20 (bottom), 25, 33 (top & bottom), 43, 44, 51 (bottom), 52, 53, 54; Veterans of Foreign Wars, 3; Robert Hunt Library, 9, 13, 15; UPI/ Bettmann, 17, 22, 29; Brown Brothers, 24; Imperial War Museum, London, 26, 27, 34, 36, 46; Historical Pictures/Stock Montage, 41; Lauros-Giraudon/Art Resources, NY, 57.

Library of Congress Cataloging-in-Publication Data

McGowen, Tom.
World War I / by Tom McGowen.
p. cm.— (A First book)
Includes bibliographical references and index.
Summary: Provides an overview of the military battles and political changes that occurred during World War I.
ISBN 0-531-20149-X   (HC : library binding)
ISBN 0-531-15660-5 (Paperback)
1. World War, 1914–1918—Juvenile literature. [1. World War, 1914–1918.] I. Title. II. Title: World War One. III. Series.
D522.7.M28 1993
940.3—dc20
92-28329 CIP AC

WORLD WAR I

CONTENTS

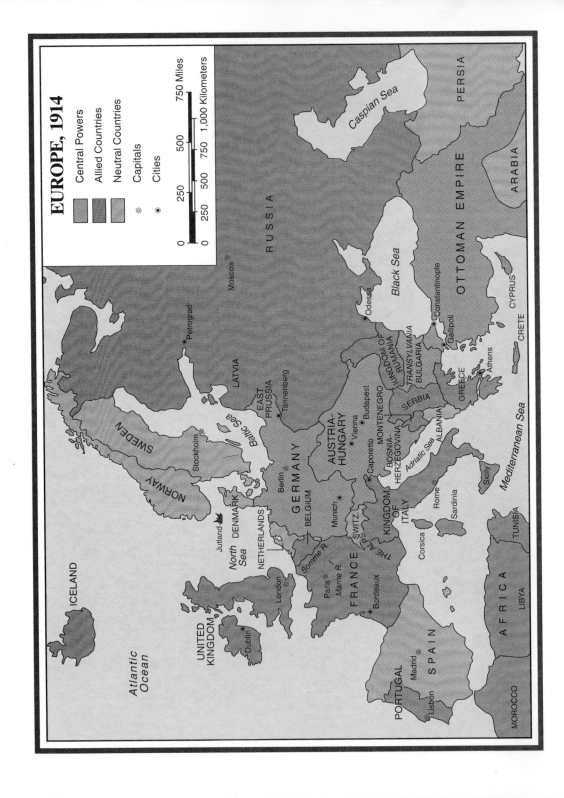

EUROPE, 1914

Central Powers
Allied Countries
Neutral Countries
⊛ Capitals
• Cities

0   250   500   750 Miles
0   250   500   750   1,000 Kilometers

ICELAND

Atlantic
Ocean

UNITED
KINGDOM
Dublin •
London •

PORTUGAL
Lisbon •

Madrid ⊛
SPAIN

MOROCCO

AFRICA
LIBYA

TUNISIA

Corsica

Sardinia

Sicily

Mediterranean Sea

NORWAY

SWEDEN

Stockholm ⊛

North
Sea

Jutland

DENMARK

NETHERLANDS

BELGIUM

Baltic Sea

Berlin ⊛

GERMANY

Munich •

SWITZ.

THE ALPS

FRANCE

Paris ⊛
Marne R.
Somme R.

Bordeaux •

KINGDOM
OF
ITALY

Rome •

Petrograd •

LATVIA

EAST
PRUSSIA

Tannenberg •

RUSSIA

Moscow ⊛

AUSTRIA-
HUNGARY

Vienna •
Budapest •

Caporetto •

MONTENEGRO

BOSNIA-
HERZEGOVINA

Adriatic Sea

ALBANIA

KINGDOM OF
RUMANIA

TRANSYLVANIA

SERBIA

BULGARIA

GREECE

Athens •

Odessa •

Black Sea

Constantinople ⊛

Gallipoli •

OTTOMAN EMPIRE

CYPRUS

CRETE

Caspian Sea

PERSIA

ARABIA

ONE

1914

IN THE YEAR 1914, most nations of Europe were still ruled by kings and emperors as they had been for centuries. There were old hatreds and enmities between many of these nations, so most of them had made treaties with friendly nations, to be assured of help and protection in the event of an attack by an enemy. The Republic of France, which feared and hated its neighbor, Germany, had a treaty with the Russian Empire (today's Russia and Commonwealth States, plus Finland and part of Poland), to go to each other's aid if one got involved in a war. Russia also had a treaty guaranteeing its protection to the little kingdom of Serbia (now Yugoslavia), which was bordered by the huge Austro-Hungarian Empire (Austria, Hungary, Croatia, Bosnia-Herzegovina, and parts of the Czech Republic and Slovakia, Poland, and Italy). Austria-Hungary had a treaty with the German Empire (Germany, plus parts of present-day Poland, The Czech Republic, Slovakia, and

France). Thus, if any one of these nations went to war, the others would surely be drawn in.

On June 28, 1914, a large green car turned up a street in the city of Sarajevo, in the Austro-Hungarian province of Bosnia. In the back seat of the open car sat a portly, mustached man in a colorful uniform, and a brightly dressed woman. This pair was the Archduke Francis Ferdinand, destined to become the next emperor of the Austro-Hungarian Empire, and his wife, Sophie.

Suddenly, a gaunt, shabby young man darted at the car, pointing a pistol. Two shots shattered the air, and the Archduke and his wife slumped in their seats, blood welling from wounds in their bodies. The man who was to have become emperor had been assassinated.

The assassin, twenty-year-old Gavrilo Princip, was a citizen of Serbia, which adjoined Bosnia. Bosnia had a large Serbian population, and there was widespread feeling in Serbia that the two countries should be united. Princip was a member of a terrorist group dedicated to bringing this about, and the Austro-Hungarian government believed that these terrorists had the secret backing of the Serbian government. The assassination now provided a way to strike at Serbia, and the Austro-Hungarians presented Serbia with an ultimatum—a list of demands which, if not agreed to, would result in a declaration of war. The demands were deliberately made so harsh that Serbia could not possibly have agreed to

French soldiers who marched off to war in 1914 wore dark
blue coats, red pants, and pale blue caps—colors that made
them highly visible targets at a long distance.

them. Knowing it could not avoid war, Serbia began
mobilization (moving its army toward the enemy border). Austria immediately did the same, and on July 28,
declared war. What was to become known as World War
I had begun.

Now, the complicated alliances binding nations to
one another came into effect. Honoring its treaty to protect Serbia, the Russian Empire began mobilizing on its
border with Austria-Hungary, and because it knew it
must fight Germany, too, it also mobilized on Germany's

eastern border. In accordance with its treaty with Russia, France mobilized on Germany's western border, and five hours later, Germany began mobilization. There was now no turning back for any of these nations.

At this time the armies of Europe were composed of infantry (foot soldiers), cavalry (soldiers on horses), and artillery. These armies had no tanks, guided missiles, very few trucks (supplies were carried in horse-drawn wagons), and only a few airplanes, used mainly for scouting out enemy forces. A foot soldier's weapon was a rifle that could fire from five to ten shots before reloading, and had an effective range of about 600 yards (549 m). Cavalrymen carried short rifles, but their main weapon was actually a sword or lance. Machine guns, of which every army had a small number, could fire around five hundred bullets a minute. Artillery cannons could fire about six explosive shells a minute, at ranges of from 2 to 5 miles (3 to 8 km). The navies of European nations were composed of coal-burning armored warships that were essentially floating platforms for large cannons. Most major navies possessed some submarines armed with torpedoes.

Armies were basically formed of units called divisions. An infantry division had about 12,000 to 13,000 riflemen, 4,000 artillerymen serving 72 or more cannons, and several thousand other men who functioned as wagon drivers, bridge builders, and so on. A cavalry

King George V of Great Britain, with some of his generals and
political leaders, inspects cannon projectiles in an English
munitions factory at the outbreak of the war.

division might have 4,000 to 9,000 men and horses and
24 cannons. Generally, two infantry divisions were
grouped together to form what was called a corps (pro-
nounced *kor*), several corps plus cavalry divisions were
grouped to form an army, and a number of armies—des-
ignated 1st Army, 2nd Army, and so on—formed the
standing army of each nation. The soldiers of these
armies began World War I in uniforms that were fairly
bright and very visible: French and Austrian troops
wore blue and red, Germans wore gray-green trimmed
with red, British and Russians wore shades of yellowish-
brown trimmed with various colors.

With enemy armies mobilizing on both its borders, the German Empire had a serious problem. But a German general, Alfred von Schlieffen, had worked out a plan for dealing with just such a two-front war. It involved sending armies through Belgium, to make a quick swing down into northwestern France to hit the French armies from the side and rear, meanwhile fighting a slow, delaying battle in the east against the Russians. German military leaders believed this would enable them to quickly knock out France, and then they could turn their full strength against Russia. Thus, on August 4, German troops marched across the Belgian border. Under still another treaty, however, the British Empire (which included Britain, Ireland, Canada, Australia, New Zealand, India, and several other countries) was bound to protect Belgium, so the British now declared war on Germany, which the Germans had not really expected.

The German forces easily pushed back the tiny, poorly equipped Belgian army and crushingly defeated French troops that had entered German border territory. But on August 17, two Russian armies moved into the German territory of East Prussia (now the northern part of Poland) and Germany found itself fighting on two fronts, as had been anticipated. From August 20 to 25, however, the German armies in Belgium forced the Belgian, French, and newly arrived British forces to steadily give way before them, while at the same time in

Dismounted German cavalrymen set up an ambush for enemy patrols in a wooded area in France. Their uniforms were grayish-green with red trim. The helmets were leather, covered with cloth.

East Prussia, German troops battled the Russian advance to a standstill. On August 26, in a swampy, forested area of East Prussia near a town called Tannenberg, German forces encircled the Russian 2nd Army and completely destroyed it. In Russian Poland, an Austro-Hungarian army was steadily pushing Russian forces back. Things appeared to be going very well for the Central Powers (Germany and Austria-Hungary) and it was beginning to look as if the war would be short and not too costly, as most "experts" had predicted, with Germany and its ally winning quickly.

But on August 29, as the German 2nd Army was moving down out of Belgium into France, the French 5th Army lashed out in a vigorous attack that stopped the Germans in their tracks. General Karl Wilhelm von Bülow, the 2nd Army's commander, called for help from General Alexander von Kluck's 1st Army, which was moving along to the right. Von Kluck ordered a wheeling movement to go to the 2nd Army's aid, a movement that swung his army east of the French capital of Paris, instead of going west, behind it, according to the Schlieffen Plan. On September 5, suddenly aware that the unguarded side of von Kluck's army was moving past it, the French 6th Army in and around Paris launched an attack that began what is known as the Battle of the Marne. Other French and British troops came to the 6th Army's aid, and for five days artillery thudded, rifles cracked, and machine guns chattered as French, British, and German soldiers battled along the Marne River. Finally, the German armies pulled back and began to dig trenches—deep ditches in which soldiers could stand and fire at opposing troops, their bodies protected from return fire by the earth.

German infantrymen in a newly dug trench. They are well-protected, and an enemy force would have to come at them over open ground, however the attackers would lose many lives in such battles.

The German Schlieffen Plan was now ruined, and all hope for a quick end to the war had vanished. In France and Belgium, the Allied (British and French) and German forces began a rapid northward movement, each trying to slip around behind the other, and each fortifying the land it passed through with trenches, leaving troops behind to occupy them.

In the east, things seemed to be going better for Germany, as its troops in East Prussia shattered the remaining Russian army there, driving it into retreat with the loss of 125,000 men. Then, on August 29, the Turkish Empire (Turkey and much of the present-day Middle East), which had made a secret treaty with the Central Powers, declared war on the Allies. This was a major development that served to cut Russia off from any help from the west and threatened it with invasion from the south. To try to take the pressure off Russia, a British army was sent to invade Mesopotamia, a part of the Turkish Empire that is now the nation of Iraq. On November 5, however, a Turkish army invaded southern Russia.

In Belgium during November, bloody battles nearly wiped out the small British force there, preventing the Germans from reaching the seacoast ahead of the Allies and capturing the coastal ports. Neither side had been able to get around the other, so by December a double

British soldiers work to extend a trench that stretches back for miles across the countryside. Lines of trenches ran for hundreds of miles across France and part of Belgium.

THE WAR, 1914

Central Powers

Allied Countries

Neutral Countries

→ German "Schlieffen Plan" to encircle Paris

→ Actual route of German armies

→ Allied counter-offensive

〵 Front line as of Winter, 1914

⊛ Capitals

⊙ Cities

North Sea

GREAT BRITAIN

IJsselmeer

Amsterdam

NETHERLANDS

The Hague

London

Rotterdam

Maas R.

Rhine R.

Essen

Dover

ENGLISH CHANNEL

Dusseldorf

Antwerp

BELGIUM

Cologne

Dunkirk

Calais

Brussels

FRANCE

Ardennes

GERMANY

Somme R.

LUXEMBOURG

Amiens

Seine R.

Cantigny

Belleau Wood

Verdun

Paris

Chateau-Thierry

Meuse R.

Seine R.

| 0 | 25 | 50 | 75 | 100 | 125 Miles |

| 0 | 25 | 50 | 75 | 100 | 125 | 150 | 175 Kilometers |

line of trenches, facing each other, ran through Belgium and France some 400 miles (643.7 km), from the North Sea down to the Swiss border. The war of movement was over in the west, and the terrible period of trench warfare began, in which soldiers were sent charging through rains of exploding artillery shells, against trenches protected by barbed wire fences and machine guns positioned to catch advancing troops in a deadly cross fire.

By the end of the first five months of the war in the west, the Allies and Germans had each lost nearly a million men, and neither side had gained its objective. In the east, East Prussia was now free of Russian invaders, but the Turkish army in Russia was bogged down in winter snows, and an Austro-Hungarian army that had invaded Serbia had been driven out. At the year's end, in both east and west, the opposing armies faced one another in sullen stalemate.

Above: Poisonous gas was a horrible weapon of World War I. These American soldiers in protective masks are moving through a cloud of gas, but one man, unable to get his mask on in time, is suffering from the searing, choking effect of the gas.

Left: A World War I gas mask.

TWO
1915

FROM JANUARY 1 to the end of March, major efforts by the French Army to regain the parts of France held by the Germans were useless. Direct attacks made on trenches by charging men had cost the French 400,000 soldiers by March 13.

In April, the Germans launched an attack in Belgium using a new weapon—poisonous gas. The gas was released from tubes placed at intervals along the line of German trenches and was blown forward by the wind in a broad greenish-yellow cloud that rolled over the ground like a thick sickly mist. It caught the French Algerian troops in its path by surprise, and shortly, German soldiers were smashing through the shocked, panic-stricken Algerians coughing in agony and completely unable to fight. But the attack was halted by the Canadian 1st Division, which had not been in the main path of the gas cloud and hurried forward to battle fiercely with rifle and machine gun fire, keeping the Germans from breaking through. Had the Germans realized how

Australian troops landing from ships near Gallipoli, Turkey.
Soon after the landing the Australians came under murderous
fire from Turkish troops in the hills.

deadly the gas would be, they might have assigned more men to the attack and scored a major victory, but this was not done and now the element of surprise in the use of this "secret weapon" was gone. The Allies quickly devised masks to protect their troops in the future, and began to produce poison gas of their own. (This horrible weapon was outlawed after the war.)

Even as the gas attack was taking place, an Allied army was moving toward a major invasion of Turkey. A narrow strip of water, the Dardanelles Strait, flows between two parts of Turkey into the Sea of Marmara, and at the far end of the sea is another strait, the Bosporus. If the Allies could gain control of the Bosporus they would have a direct water route to Russia, through which troops and supplies could be sent. So, in the early morning darkness of April 25, British, French, Australian, and New Zealand troops were landed from boats on a long stretch of Turkish coast along the Dardanelles, near the town of Gallipoli. Their goal was to storm quickly inland and seize high ground, but the invasion was poorly planned, poorly handled—and the Turks were expecting it. Allied troops began to drop by the dozens under the impact of murderous crackling machine gun fire from the heights beyond the beach. Desperately, the Allied force began to dig in, and there was soon a trench running along the beach, just like the trenches in France. The invasion was a failure.

Since early February, Germany had been waging submarine warfare against merchant ships of all nations in the seas around Britain, attempting to cut off the flow of supplies to the island. On May 7, a German submarine torpedoed the British passenger ship *Lusitania* off the Irish coast, causing the deaths of 1,198 people, 128 of whom were Americans. There was worldwide outrage, and the United States sent an angry protest to Germany. German-American relations, which had been fairly good at the start of the war, were now seriously hurt.

The *Lusitania*, shown leaving from New York for the voyage to Britain on which she was torpedoed and sunk by a German submarine.

German submarines in a north-German harbor. These
vessels attacked and sunk many ships of neutral
(not in the war) nations, arousing anger against
Germany, especially in America.

Above: Canadian troops go "over the top" of their trench to
make an attack on the German trench opposite them. Such
attacks generally caused enormous losses for the attackers.

Opposite page: Emerging from a narrow trench, a raiding
party of British soldiers heads into the "no man's land"
between their trench and the enemy's trench.

Throughout May and June, British and French forces in France continued to assault the German trenches in attempts to gain back even small bits of captured land. Thousands of men would surge forward across the "no man's land" between the two rows of trenches, dropping by the hundreds beneath the storm of exploding artillery shells and the slicing sweep of bullets from the machine guns. The surviving solders could only turn and rush back to the safety of their trenches, with absolutely nothing gained but an enormous, terrible loss of life.

In the east, however, the war was still one of movement, and on May 2, German forces launched an attack in Russian Poland that sent the Russian army reeling back. But the Central Powers were dealt a serious blow when, on May 23, the Kingdom of Italy entered the war on the Allied side, declaring war on the Austro-Hungarian Empire, which held some territory the Italians regarded as rightfully theirs and which had been promised to them by the Allied governments in a secret treaty. The Italians began to make assaults on Austrian frontier defenses in the mountains that bordered the two countries, but were easily beaten back.

From June through July, the advance of combined German-Austrian forces in Poland continued. The entire Russian front began to collapse, the Russians in head-long retreat, unable to check the enemy advance. During this same period of time, the Allied troops at Gallipoli grimly hung on in their trenches while their leaders debated what to do. In August they were reinforced by three fresh divisions, and an attempt was made to storm inland and capture the heights. In blistering heat, men struggled forward through a deadly downpour of artillery shells and a continuous sheet of rifle and machine gun fire. The attack was a bloody failure.

On August 9, another British passenger ship was sunk by a German submarine, and four Americans were among those killed. Reaction from the United States was so hostile that the German kaiser (emperor) felt it necessary to announce a halt to submarine warfare.

In September, autumn rains turned the Polish roads into stretches of mud, and the German-Austrian advance

Australian troops on a transport ship wait to land at
Gallipoli to take part in a major attack on the Turkish
positions in the hills. The attack was a dreadful failure.

bogged down. But the Central Powers' forces had gained 300 miles (482 km), inflicted more than one million casualties on the Russians, and captured 90,000 prisoners. This success convinced the little Kingdom of Bulgaria to take the Central Powers' side, and on October 6, German, Austro-Hungarian, and Bulgarian armies invaded Serbia from three sides. Throughout October and November, the outnumbered and poorly supplied Serbian army steadily retreated, finally leaving Serbia altogether and straggling through the tiny neighboring countries of Montenegro and Albania, to the coast of the Adriatic Sea. There, the ragged survivors were picked up by French and Italian ships. Serbia, as well as Montenegro, was occupied by Central Powers' forces.

At Gallipoli, the invasion had been given up and the Allied troops were evacuated. They had taken more than 250,000 casualties and had accomplished nothing. In Mesopotamia, the advance of the British army had been stopped by strong Turkish resistance, and the British were forced to retreat back to the town of Kut al Amara, which was quickly surrounded by Turkish forces. Thus, for the Allies, the last days of 1915 were bleak. For the Central Powers, things seemed more promising, and the German commander, General Erich von Falkenhayn, spent his Christmas working out a plan that he believed could destroy the French Army and end the war in the west.

GENERAL VON FALKENHAYN'S plan was simply to launch an attack at some place the French Army would feel it had to defend with every last soldier. Thus, said Falkenhayn, the French forces would bleed themselves dry and have to surrender. With their French allies out of the war, the British would have to make peace. Germany could then turn its full attention to beating Russia and ending the war.

The place Falkenhayn picked to attack was the French city of Verdun, which was surrounded by forts. If Verdun were captured, the road to Paris would be wide open, so the French would do anything to prevent its capture.

Early on the morning of February 21, French troops at one of the key forts were suddenly engulfed by a shattering storm of flame and explosions as German artillery opened a ten-hour long barrage. Then, hordes of German infantry came pouring through the shell-shattered remains of the woods around the fort. After a long vicious struggle in which the Germans made use of a horrible new weapon, the flamethrower, the French dropped back. This was the beginning of the ten-month Battle of Verdun—a nightmare of attacks, counterattacks, and titanic artillery barrages causing enormous casualties on both sides, turning vast acres of forest into a virtual desert, and just about demolishing Verdun itself.

It became a bad spring for the Allies. In March the Russian army started a drive in Poland that bogged down and was hurled back with a loss of 70,000 to 100,000 casualties. On April 29, the British troops trapped in Kut al Amara, Mesopotamia, were forced to surrender. And on May 15, the Austrians struck with a surprise offensive against the Italians in the border region of Trentino, inflicting 177,000 casualties.

Since the beginning of the war, most of the German naval fleet had been kept in ports, in the hope of tying down the stronger British fleet by forcing it to stay close to the German ports lest German ships try to sneak out. Now, on May 31, the German High Seas Fleet, ninety-nine ships, glided out of its harbors with the objective of carrying out a plan to catch a portion of the British fleet by itself and destroy it. But the British picked up German radio messages and suspected that the Germans were coming, so the entire British Grand Fleet, 151 ships strong, steamed forth to intercept them.

Top: For ten months, French and German troops fought a continuous battle around the French city of Verdun. The city was reduced to shattered ruins by steady artillery fire.

Right: French soldiers defending Verdun lived through almost constant artillery bombardment and frequent assaults by German troops. Both sides had hundreds of thousands of men killed and wounded.

This painting depicts a moment in the Battle of Jutland,
1916, between the British and German battle fleets.
This was one of the biggest naval battles of history, but
it made no difference in the war.

The battle that began at 3:30 that afternoon, in a region of the North Sea known as Jutland Bank, was one of the largest sea battles in history. From late afternoon until early morning darkness of the next day, the big guns of the ships thundered over the water. A German shell exploded in the powder compartment of the British battleship *Indefatigable*, and with a titanic explosion the *Indefatigable* blew up. The battleship *Queen Mary* was nearly split in half and sank in minutes. The German battleship *Pommern* was struck by torpedoes from three destroyers and went down, and the battleship *Lutzow* was so badly damaged it had to be abandoned. By dawn, aware that their plan had failed, the Germans withdrew and returned to their ports. They had lost 11 ships and 2,545 sailors; the British lost 14 ships and 6,097 men. Technically, it was a German victory, but the British fleet was still far stronger, and the German fleet never again attempted to leave harbor.

To take pressure off the Italians, reeling from the hard-hitting Austrian offensive at Trentino in May, four Russian armies moved in an offensive in Austrian Poland on June 4, rolling back the outnumbered Austrian forces. This had an effect on things in the west; fifteen German divisions were taken away from the armies fighting the Battle of Verdun, and were sent to help the Austro-Hungarian troops in Poland.

On July 1, the British, with some French help, began a large-scale attack along the Somme River in northwest France. Bitter fighting raged throughout July, with little result except that some German troops were pulled away from Verdun to bolster the German forces fighting in the Battle of the Somme. In September, the British made a new assault that introduced a new weapon, the tank. They made sizeable gains, but no breakthrough as had been hoped the tanks could accomplish, and the Somme offensive petered out. British losses had been 420,000 men, French were 195,000, German were 650,000.

British tanks in action for the first time, in the Battle of the Somme. They got the name "tanks" because the crates they were shipped to France in were marked "Water Tanks" in an effort to keep their real purpose secret.

By mid–1916, the appearance of most armies had greatly changed. Most soldiers, except for the Russians, were now wearing a steel helmet that protected a man's head from the metal balls and fragments that were hurled through the air by the explosion of an artillery shell. The blue and red French uniforms had been replaced by pale blue ones that blended into the background, and Austrian uniforms were now pale gray.

There had also been changes in weapons. Armies now had hundreds of scouting planes that were armed with machine guns and fought one another for control of the sky. Bombing planes had been developed, and air raids on enemy supply areas, docks, and cities had become commonplace. The city of London had been bombed many times by zeppelins, huge lighter-than-air crafts similar to the blimps of today. Both sides were now using poison gas, and when the British tanks showed what they could do, both France and Germany began producing tanks.

In the autumn, at Verdun, with the Germans now weakened by having to send troops to Poland and the Somme, the French army lashed out in an offensive. By December 18, French troops had regained most of the territory lost since February, which was now a muddy desolation of shell holes, shattered tree stumps, and thousands of unburied dead. In the ten months of fighting the French had lost 542,000 men and the Germans 434,000.

Above: The testing of the first zeppelin, a lighter-than-aircraft like a modern blimp, in Germany in 1907. During World War I, Germany used zeppelins to bomb London and other targets.

Right: World War I was the first war in which combat between airplanes took place.

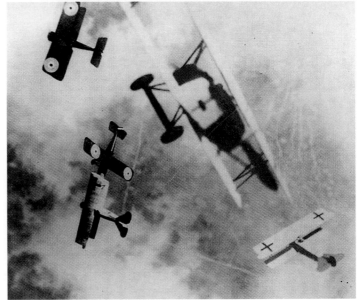

Verdun had been a useless, wasteful effort, but elsewhere the German armies had scored major victories. In September, the Russian offensive in Poland was turned back as the German troops from Verdun went into action. The Russian offensive had nearly knocked the Austro-Hungarian Empire out of the war, but Germany had enabled it to survive, and now it was the Russians who were in trouble.

Germany scored another victory in the Kingdom of Rumania. On August 27, impressed by the early success of the Russian offensive in Poland, Rumania declared war on the Central Powers and invaded Hungarian Transylvania, which it coveted. But a German army drove the invaders back into Rumania and then, linking up with a German-Bulgarian force, inflicted a crushing defeat that destroyed the Russian army. By the year's end, Rumania was occupied by German forces, and its rich grain and oil fields were providing food and fuel for Germany and its armies.

And Russia, with millions of dead, racked by shortages of food, fuel, and medicines, and with most of its soldiers and citizens demanding an end to the war, was on the verge of collapse and revolution.

GERMAN MILITARY leaders had come to the conclusion that if all supplies to Britain could be cut off, Britain would face starvation and economic collapse, and would be forced to ask for peace within five months. So, on January 31, German submarines again began unrestricted warfare in the waters around Britain. The German forces in France and Belgium went on the defensive, pulling back to a new, shorter and more easily defended line of trenches some 20 miles (32 km) behind the old lines. Germany was now prepared to just hold off any attacks and simply wait for the British Empire to collapse.

Germany's decision to unleash submarines against the ships of neutral (not in the war) nations, however, caused the United States and several other countries to break off relations with the German Empire. Sure that the United States would soon enter the war, Germany tried to take steps to block the Americans by attempting to persuade Mexico to side with Germany and make war on the United States. When Americans learned of this there was a wave of outrage, and when, in March, three American ships were torpedoed by German submarines, it was the last straw. On April 6, the United States declared war. There were only 110,000 men in its army, however, so it needed to do a great deal of building up.

Allied military operations in the spring of the year were split between successes and failures. In the Near East, a new British army in Mesopotamia drove the Turks out of the region, and another British army invaded the Turkish territory of Palestine (now Israel). But a

Upon entering the war, the United States had to quickly build up its armed forces. Recruiting posters such as this helped bring men into the army.

huge attack, made against the new German lines in France by a gigantic French force of 1.2 million men, was a colossal failure. One hundred eighty thousand French soldiers were killed and wounded by German artillery and machine guns while charging across open ground. Angered that their leaders continued to use such stupid, suicidal tactics, thousands of French soldiers mutinied—rioting, throwing away their weapons, deserting, refusing to obey orders. The mutiny was ruthlessly stopped by the French commanders, who had many men executed.

The Central Powers, already facing the threat of a new enemy when U.S. troops arrived in Europe, found themselves facing yet another opponent in early summer. The King of Greece, who favored the Central Powers, was deposed, and his place was taken by his pro-Allied son, Alexander. On July 2, Greece entered the war on the Allied side, and the Greek army joined with a small Allied force that had been sent to the area, to move against the Central Powers' ally, Bulgaria.

On March 20, the long-feared revolt had finally broken out in Russia, with crowds rioting in Petrograd. Troops began to mutiny. The czar (emperor) gave up the throne and a new government was formed, which pledged to continue the war with better leadership. But the breakdown of discipline in the army and navy continued, with officers being murdered and men deserting.

The first American troops to reach France disembarked at
the port of St. Nazaire in June 1917. They had to depend
on the French and British for much of their weapons and
equipment, such as helmets and artillery.

On July 1, Russian troops in Poland, on orders from the new government, launched a major offensive. Caught by surprise at first, the German and Austro-Hungarian forces gave ground, but then they stiffened and brought the Russian attack to a halt. On July 19, reinforced by German troops, the German and Austrian armies counter-attacked and the Russian force disintegrated. Revolution spread in Russia, with the Bolsheviks (communists), who were opposed to the war, gaining the support of many people. On September 1, a German army struck northward into Russian Latvia, driving the Russian forces there back in panic. Russia now dis-

In March 1917, revolution broke out in the city of Petrograd, Russia. Mobs of soldiers thronged the streets, calling for an end to the rule of the czar (emperor). By November, Russia was out of the war.

solved in chaos with the Bolsheviks seizing full power. By November, the Bolshevik leaders were seeking to make peace with Germany. Although it did not officially surrender until March 3, 1918, Russia was now out of the war.

This left the Central Powers' armies in the east free to concentrate on Italy. On October 24, following an artillery barrage of poison gas shells, German and Austrian troops smashed through the Italian defenses in the rugged mountainous region of the Alps near the town of Caporetto. The Italians collapsed in panic, falling back some 80 miles (128 km), with losses of about 45,000 casualties, 275,000 prisoners, and untold amounts of supplies and equipment. Italy was on the brink of being knocked out of the war, and British and French troops were rushed to its aid by ship.

But while things were going badly for the Allies in Europe, they were going well in the Near East. The British army in Palestine captured the important city of Beersheba, breaking through the Turkish entrenchments around the city with a wild charge of thousands of cavalrymen. Then, moving quickly, the British split the Turkish forces in two, driving them into headlong retreat.

Despite this good news, Allied leaders were grim and worried. Italy was in serious trouble and the loss of Russia was a devastating blow. French and British armies had been weakened badly by bloody, costly offen-

Thousands of Turkish prisoners of war, guarded by British soldiers,
trudge through the streets of Baghdad following a tremendous
British victory in Mesopotamia (Iraq).

sives, and a vigorous German attack might crumple them. There were doubts whether American troops would reach Europe before it was too late.

The military leaders of the Central Powers were also gravely concerned. Although the victory over Russia was tremendously helpful, and the situation in Italy seemed promising, the Austro-Hungarian Empire was near collapse, Turkey appeared to be crumbling, and Bulgaria was now threatened. And there was also the certain knowledge that Germany's weakened and weary troops in France would soon be facing a fresh new army when the Americans arrived.

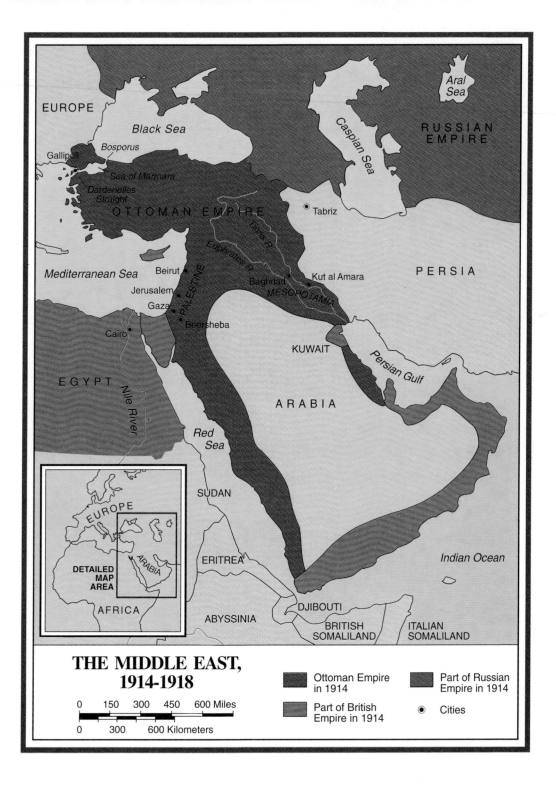

EUROPE

Black Sea

Bosporus

Gallipoli

Sea of Marmara

Dardanelles
Straight

OTTOMAN EMPIRE

Tabriz

Aral
Sea

RUSSIAN
EMPIRE

Caspian Sea

Euphrates R.

Tigris R.

Mediterranean Sea

Beirut

PALESTINE

Jerusalem

Gaza

Beersheba

Baghdad

MESOPOTAMIA

Kut al Amara

PERSIA

Cairo

EGYPT

Nile River

KUWAIT

Persian Gulf

ARABIA

Red
Sea

Indian Ocean

SUDAN

DETAILED
MAP
AREA

EUROPE

ARABIA

AFRICA

ERITREA

ABYSSINIA

DJIBOUTI

BRITISH
SOMALILAND

ITALIAN
SOMALILAND

THE MIDDLE EAST,
1914-1918

| 0 | 150 | 300 | 450 | 600 Miles |

| 0 | 300 | 600 Kilometers |

Ottoman Empire
in 1914

Part of British
Empire in 1914

Part of Russian
Empire in 1914

⊙ Cities

FIVE

1918

AT THE BEGINNING of 1918, Germany possessed a slight numerical advantage over the French and British in the west, about 194 divisions to 173. But once American forces reached Europe and entered into combat, the Allies would have overwhelming strength. So, the German high command had determined that their only hope lay in gaining a decisive victory over France and Britain before U.S. troops became a factor. With Russia now out of the war and Italy in disarray, the Germans felt they could safely pull most of their troops out of the east, and began bringing them to the western front, France and Belgium, building up the forces there for a major assault.

By March 21, everything was ready, and three German armies were prepared to launch an offensive that was designed to split the British force away from the French and destroy it completely, which would leave France no choice but to make peace before the

German artillerymen study the countryside through a
range-finder, preparing to begin a barrage that will launch
the giant German offensive of 1918. Despite early success,
the German effort ended in failure.

Americans arrived. Following a short artillery barrage of high explosive shells and poison gas, the Germans began an advance that broke through one British army and went some 40 miles (64 km) before they were finally stopped on April 5, mainly by French troops that were rushed to the aid of the British. The Germans had inflicted 150,000 casualties and captured 90,000 prisoners and more than 2,000 cannons. It was a strong gain, but the Germans had not accomplished what they had hoped.

They quickly struck again, on April 9, with an offensive aimed at the British lines in Belgium, near the seacoast. In two days, they scored a 10-mile (16-km) advance, but then British resistance stiffened, and by the 29th this offensive, too, was halted with no real result.

An American force of more than 300,000 men, commanded by Major General John Pershing, was now in France, and when the Germans launched still another offensive, on May 27, American soldiers saw combat. On the 28th, the U.S. 1st Division attacked a strongly fortified German position at the French town of Cantigny. The Americans captured the town, then beat off repeated counterattacks by veteran German shock troops. Meanwhile, the U.S. 2nd and 3rd Divisions were rushed to the aid of French troops battling to stop the German advance that had penetrated 30 miles (42 km), to the Marne River. The 3rd Division was put in position to

Top: American soldiers, who were
known as "doughboys," warily
examine a ruined farmhouse for
lurking German troops.

Right: A weary doughboy rests in
a crater made by an artillery shell
(projectile) explosion, which he
has lined with empty shell casings
and cartridge boxes.

Above: The shattered French town of Chateau Thierry, captured
from German forces by American troops. Many French and Belgian towns
suffered similar devastation.

Opposite page: This area of Belleau Woods, where German and American forces
waged a vicious battle, shows the effect of warfare on a once lovely forest—
dead, smashed trees and the remains of a picturesque hunting lodge.

defend bridges that crossed the river at the town of
Chateau-Thierry; it held the bridges against a number of
assaults, then made a counterattack that hurled the
Germans back. West of Chateau-Thierry, in the forested
area of Belleau Wood, the 2nd Division fought off an
attack, then also counterattacked and forced the Germans
to withdraw. These successes by inexperienced troops
against combat-hardened veterans were greatly encour-
aging to the British and French, and deeply disturbing to
the Germans.

In the remains of a forest near the Marne River in
France, French soldiers look over a trench abandoned by
the Germans in their 1918 retreat.

This third German offensive, however, had put a 30-mile (42-km) dent into the Allied lines, and seeing a possibility to burst the dent open and finally achieve a breakthrough, the German commander, General Erich Ludendorff, struck with yet a fourth offensive on June 9. But the French commanders were expecting this and had prepared for it, and by the 13th it had been repulsed. The Germans continued to batter desperately at the Allied lines with two attacks in July, but both were stopped within a few days. Since the beginning of the first offensive in March, the Germans had lost more than half a million men.

By late July, there were more than twenty-five American divisions in France, and the Allies felt confident enough to launch an offensive of their own. French and American troops attacked the Germans along the Marne River, rolling them back and wiping out all the gains they had made since March. On August 8th, British and French forces struck the Germans in the north, catching them by surprise and pushing them all the way back to their original starting point. Everything the German offensives had gained had now been taken back, and the German effort had all been for nothing. General Ludendorff now felt it was no longer possible for Germany to win the war, and advised the German government to try to make peace with the Allies.

Things now began to move swiftly to a conclusion. On September 12, the U.S. 1st Army attacked the last German-held position in northern France, in the area of the town of St. Mihiel, taking it on the 16th with the capture of 15,000 prisoners. Two days later, the Allied army in Greece marched into Serbia and attacked the Bulgarian army there, shattering it. On the 29th, Bulgaria signed an armistice (an agreement to stop fighting) with the Allies, and was out of the war. Even as these victories were taking place in eastern and western Europe, the British army in Palestine struck successive blows at the Turkish 4th, 7th, and 8th armies, routing them.

By the end of October, the finish was in sight. In Germany, there was now starvation and a breakdown of law and order, with many cities seized by revolutionary groups of communists. In Italy, Italian, British, and French troops made an attack that split the Austrian line open, and Austrian resistance began to collapse. On October 30, no longer able to stand against the British, Turkey signed an armistice and dropped out of the war. Four days later, Austria gave up.

In Germany, revolutionary forces took over the government and proclaimed the German nation a republic. The kaiser fled into Holland. On November 11, Germany's representatives met with the French Army commander, Marshal Ferdinand Foch, agreed to surren-

Allied generals, admirals, and politicians meet to discuss the surrender terms for Germany in this painting of the meeting. The harsh surrender terms imposed on Germany may well have helped to cause World War II twenty years later.

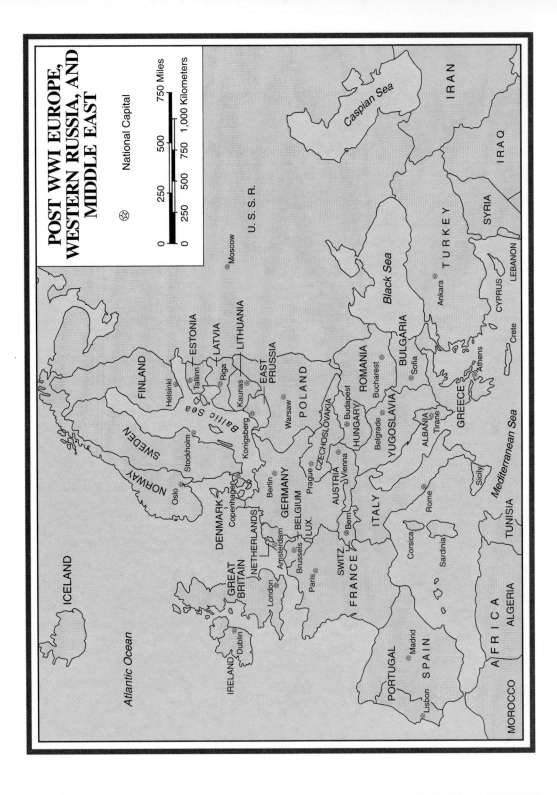

POST WWI EUROPE, WESTERN RUSSIA, AND MIDDLE EAST

National Capital
⊛

0   250   500   750 Miles
0 250 500 750 1,000 Kilometers

IRAN

Caspian Sea

IRAQ

U. S. S. R.

TURKEY

SYRIA

LEBANON

⊛ Moscow

Ankara ⊛

CYPRUS

Black Sea

Crete

ESTONIA
LATVIA
LITHUANIA

FINLAND

EAST
PRUSSIA

BULGARIA

GREECE

Tallinn
Riga
Kaunas

Helsinki

Sofia ⊛

Athens ⊛

POLAND

ROMANIA

Königsberg

Warsaw ⊛

Bucharest ⊛

SWEDEN

Baltic Sea

Stockholm ⊛

HUNGARY
YUGOSLAVIA

ALBANIA

Budapest ⊛

Belgrade ⊛

Tirane ⊛

NORWAY

Oslo ⊛

Berlin ⊛

Prague ⊛

CZECHOSLOVAKIA

Vienna ⊛

DENMARK

Copenhagen ⊛

GERMANY

AUSTRIA

ITALY

Mediterranean Sea

BELGIUM

Bern ⊛

Rome ⊛

NETHERLANDS

Amsterdam ⊛

LUX.

SWITZ.

Sicily

TUNISIA

GREAT
BRITAIN

Brussels ⊛

Paris ⊛

FRANCE

Corsica

ICELAND

London ⊛

Sardinia

Atlantic Ocean

IRELAND

Dublin ⊛

PORTUGAL

Madrid ⊛

SPAIN

A F R I C A

ALGERIA

Lisbon ⊛

MOROCCO

der terms, and signed an armistice. World War I had come to an end.

During the course of the war more than 8 million soldiers had been killed in battle, more than 21 million had been injured, and more than 6 million civilians had died. With the exception of the British Empire, all the European Empires—German, Austro-Hungarian, Russian, and Turkish—were shattered and gone, and new, very different nations such as The Czech Republic, Slovakia, and Iraq were formed out of their ruins. Poland, which had been divided between Germany, Austria-Hungary, and Russia, was reunited as an independent nation. The map of Europe became much like it is today.

The war saw the emergence of communism as a new major political force in the world, and the emergence of the United States as a new major world power. But it left Europe exhausted and in ruins. Its outcome, particularly the harsh terms imposed by France on Germany, actually led to World War II.

FOR FURTHER READING

Brooman, Josh, editor. *Great War: The First World War, 1914–18.* White Plains, NY: Longman, 1985.

Bosco, Peter. *World War I.* New York: Facts on File, 1991.

Humble, Richard. *World War I Battleship.* New York: Franklin Watts, 1989.

Matthews, Rupert. *Attack on the Lusitania.* New York: Franklin Watts, 1989.

Maynard, Christopher & David Jeffris. *The Aces: Pilots and Planes of World War I.* New York: Franklin Watts, 1987.

Ross, Stewart. *War in the Trenches: World War I.* New York: Franklin Watts, 1991.

Tames, Richard. *1900–1919.* New York: Franklin Watts, 1991.

INDEX

ABOUT THE AUTHOR

TOM McGOWEN was born in 1927 and vividly remembers that the toys, books, and films of his childhood were heavily influenced by World War I. He grew up with an intense interest in military history, and eventually served in the U.S. Navy in World War II. In his war books for juvenile readers, he says he attempts to help readers understand that battles and campaigns were fought for a specific purpose, or strategy, and did not simply "happen."

Mr. McGowen, who lives in Norridge, Illinois, is the author of forty books, including eleven written for Franklin Watts. His most recent Franklin Watts First Book was *The Korean War.* In 1986, his book *Radioactivity: From the Curies to the Atomic Age* (Franklin Watts) was named an NSTA-CBC Outstanding Science Trade Book For Children. Mr. McGowen also won the 1990 Children's Reading Roundtable Award for Outstanding Contribution to the Field of Juvenile Literature.